IN THE
NATIONAL INTEREST

General Sir John Monash once exhorted a graduating class to 'equip yourself for life, not solely for your own benefit but for the benefit of the whole community'. At the university established in his name, we repeat this statement to our own graduating classes, to acknowledge how important it is that common or public good flows from education.

Universities spread and build on the knowledge they acquire through scholarship in many ways, well beyond the transmission of this learning through education. It is a necessary part of a university's role to debate its findings, not only with other researchers and scholars, but also with the broader community in which it resides.

Publishing for the benefit of society is an important part of a university's commitment to free intellectual inquiry. A university provides civil space for such inquiry by its scholars, as well as for investigations by public intellectuals and expert practitioners.

This series, In the National Interest, embodies Monash University's mission to extend knowledge and encourage informed debate about matters of great significance to Australia's future.

Professor Margaret Gardner AC
President and Vice-Chancellor,
Monash University

JILL
HENNESSY
RESPECT

MONASH
UNIVERSITY
PUBLISHING

Monash University Publishing
Matheson Library Annexe
40 Exhibition Walk
Monash University
Clayton, Victoria 3800, Australia
https://publishing.monash.edu

Monash University Publishing brings to the world publications which advance the best traditions of humane and enlightened thought.

ISBN: 9781922464576 (paperback)
ISBN: 9781922464583 (ebook)

Series: In the National Interest
Editor: Louise Adler
Project manager & copyeditor: Paul Smitz
Designer: Peter Long
Typesetter: Cannon Typesetting
Proofreader: Gillian Armitage
Printed in Australia by Ligare Book Printers

A catalogue record for this book is available from the National Library of Australia.

To Lily-Rose and Ginger Joan.
My gifts to the world.

RESPECT

After a particularly bruising encounter in parliament, you sometimes hear male politicians say they would like to see a kinder, gentler debate. I would settle for a bit more respect thanks, especially given we spend most of our time arguing over the big three: sex, death and footy.

From where I sit as a Member of the Legislative Assembly in Spring Street, the doors of Melbourne's most prominent cathedral, abortion clinic and footy ground are no more than a short stroll away, forming a kind of crown atop the city's central business district. Pilgrims generally make their way in peace to St Patrick's and the Melbourne Cricket Ground, but up until 2019 there was no such peace for a woman walking into the abortion clinic in East Melbourne. Instead, she would be subjected to vile harassment and grotesque imagery from people offering what they considered counselling—intended to guide her back onto the path of wholesome womanhood, they'd say. This abhorrent practice had persisted for decades right under the noses of parliamentarians before the Daniel Andrews' Labor government decided that these women deserved the same respect as a follower of Jesus or the Western Bulldogs, or both.

As the minister for health at the time, and responsible for the bill to secure 'safe access zones' for women going to the clinic, I was duty-bound to listen to people and groups that had an interest in the matter, to make sure that whatever parliament ultimately made into law was tethered to community views on what was fair and right. You would have thought this one was a no-brainer, but it took literally hundreds of meetings to achieve, many of them crammed into my windowless office in the bowels of Victoria's Parliament House between the ringing of bells to mark another vote.

Most made their points in respectful tones, including a few who were keen to use the debate about access zones as a proxy to roll back the clock and ban abortions again after parliament had made them legal in 2008. But one meeting stands out, with a church leader. After rehashing his arguments, he could see that I wasn't for turning, which prompted a resigned sigh and the revelation that I had apparently lost my way morally. Respect had left the room, assuming it had ever been there. Happily, the bill was easily passed shortly after that little chat, offering some decency to those women who want to access a legal health service without being demonised practically within earshot of parliament.

We do not really need to hear more stories like that, much less the recent allegations of sexual violence and disrespect arising in our nation's capital, to know that we must elevate the role that respect plays in our public debates to match that of our personal relationships, but we can capitalise on these stories and use them to forge lasting change. These days, clashing footy crowds are more respectful of each other than those of us tussling over how policy and institutions should respond to wrongdoing. We need to catch up.

It sounds obvious, but the fact that we are even talking about this means we have lost our way. Depressingly, most would readily agree that there is a lack of mutual respect among the people engaged in our political process—that adequate attention is often not shown to those calling out racism in sport, or to survivors of sexual assault, or to those seeking gender and sexual equality, or to those who remind us that science and expertise have way more to offer than self-serving superstition.

In looking for ways to heighten the role of respect in public debate, there is cause for optimism, albeit from a most unlikely source—the discussion over how much control we should have over how our own lives end. The path we took in Victoria towards establishing laws enabling voluntary assisted dying showed how people can engage with what is to many the most meaningful and impactful personal issue, without losing sight of the right of others to hold a different view. This may be because dying is everyone's business, ultimately. The long days and nights of parliamentary debate over those laws followed even longer days and nights spent listening to a community fed up with watching loved ones die in terrible but avoidable pain, and those afraid of what giving people more agency could lead to.

Similar to the debate over safe access zones, my office, along with the offices of the other cross-party supporters who helped get the ball rolling on this reform, became congested with lobbyists making their case. This time, though, there was real respect in the exchanges. Even those with the strongest objections to the idea knew of people who nursed pain long after the dreadful drawn-out death of a loved one. Even the meetings with religious leaders who objected to the bill were different. One asked for a private chat knowing he could not persuade me to his point of view, but he nonetheless wanted to talk more broadly about the value of life, and our respective conceptions of pain and suffering. The civility of that exchange has influenced the way in which I have approached other issues of public policy ever since.

After all the lobbyists had left, what persuaded my colleagues were the voices of the gravely ill themselves, those who wanted a better end for others in the future. These brave people showed the parliament that the community had moved ahead, and it was time to align the laws with their expectations. It is the individuals who use their voices to stand up to power, staring down dogma and scepticism, who best remind us of the need to respect each other in debate—be they the gravely ill who want a better death, or Brittany Higgins holding a toxic workplace to account, or Héritier Lumumba rejecting racism on the footy field, or a public health official demonstrating how to wear a mask so as to give us all the strongest chance of stopping a pandemic.

By taking their lead, we can make respect everyone's business when it comes to debating the big issues.

EMPATHY IS NOT A WEAKNESS

To respect another means to have due regard for their feelings, wishes or rights. It means empathising with others. Empathy should not be seen as a 'soft' skill, a weakness, an attribute that crescendoed when emotional intelligence, the latest in a long line of management theories, had its moment in the sun. Empathy is instead a strength, and a key part of a public culture of respect. We can all use this to challenge and acknowledge our own biases, empowering us to try and understand other people. But a widespread desire to do this, and the presence of leadership that helps us invoke our better selves, seem to be in short supply. Worse, an attitude of deliberate disrespect and the sidelining of empathy have taken hold in this country.

Placing great value on respect and empathy is critical to ensure everyone can fully and safely engage in human progress, whether on the battle-field of parliament or that of the challenging online world that often forces facts to fight too hard to be included in the debates that erupt. The climate change wars, the anti-vaccination movement, the quarrels over COVID-19 infection controls—all show a disregard for science and expertise. Respect does not mean that ideas, arguments or political movements should be completely free from criticism or scrutiny. It is just that its absence can dehumanise people—disrespect corrodes us all. It causes the retreat from the public, policy and political spheres, however amorphous these are now as distinct spaces, of people who are smart and decent, who have important things to share and teach, who make us uncomfortable in order to confront an awkward reality. It loosens our connection with those whose help we so desperately need to solve our biggest challenges.

We rarely celebrate those who lead with great empathy and respect. My own experience in a state government that has tackled many controversial social policy issues has been that you need leaders who are prepared to go out and argue their case every single day in a way that demonstrates the purpose, the science and the humanity of a policy proposition.

New York Times staff writer Claire Cain Miller explains empathy as follows:

> It's understanding how others feel and being compassionate toward them. It happens when two parts of the brain work together, neuro-scientists say—the emotional center perceives the feelings of others and the cognitive center tries to understand why they feel that way and how we can be helpful to them.[1]

But the dominant fight-or-flight instincts of contemporary politics and the sheer speed of the media and political cycles make it difficult for even the most nobly motivated to display empathy, to do as the neuroscientists describe. It can be hard to find the space and time to really think about the feelings of others, let alone contemplate how to use policy levers to raise empathy or participate in a debate about how we can all be more helpful and caring.

I know many will expect that this is the bread and butter of politics. But the pressure and the desire to pivot out of politically awkward moments, the partisan calculus that is swiftly done, all fertilise the conditions for disrespect. The demand for immediate answers to complex problems makes it tough for public leaders to maintain the attention needed to work through the opportunities and costs of varying responses to issues. Our dismissal of anything that is too academic, coupled with the binary nature of daily politics and the general online and social media brouhaha, also mean that when the green shoots of respect do poke up through the cracks, it is mostly just too hard for them to survive.

We urgently need to find a reliable centre of gravity for respect in public life. We need to demand it for others as much as for ourselves, to not just receive it but to give it. We must graciously acknowledge it when it is displayed by those with whom we disagree. We must honour those who teach it through practice, react to its absence in a way that tenaciously supports its return, and refuse to give up on the seemingly impossible task of growing these habits in the online world. We need to catch ourselves when we individually and collectively fail.

EXHAUSTED BY OUTRAGE

It was a year we thought could not get any worse. But 2020, overshadowed as it was by COVID-19 and its implications, by the US election and its riotous aftermath, kept giving us a stream of horrifying stories and revelations, illuminating how base we can be in how we treat each other. It showed us the tenuous role that the concept of respect plays in our social contract. Were we always this awful to each other? Were we always so content to quickly move on from terrible examples of racism and sexism, so desperate to leave behind any outrage? Are we so exhausted and frightened by COVID that we lack the energy to demand better, to confront the aggregate impact of it all and decide that this is not who we want to be?

Judging by the events of early 2021, it seems to be so. The abuse of women is still a mainstream workplace experience and no-one seems to be accountable for it. The fact that one of the starkest examples of recent times happened at the so-called pinnacle of Australian politics and public law-making, our Commonwealth Parliament, is a depressing example of how the protections of government are mainly applied to protect the government. But fissures have also appeared in non-political Australian institutions.

An independent inquiry triggered by the treatment of former Australian Football League player Héritier Lumumba identified a culture of systemic racism at the Collingwood Football Club. The issue was only highlighted when, after the inquiry's findings were leaked to the media in January 2021, omnipresent Collingwood president Eddie McGuire translated this into a 'historic and proud day' for the club.[2] A week later, when an eruption of condemnation led to his resignation, he claimed that this comment had been misconstrued. But the truth was that it was not what many had wanted to hear from a leader with the responsibility to drive acceptance and change. It was disrespectful to so many, especially those who had been subjected to racism at the Collingwood FC. The club's hierarchy had failed to recognise how impossible it feels to many to make a complaint, to challenge the structures of power. This very act asks victims to carry the load, with a career-limiting price to pay for blowing the whistle.

The report of the 'Do Better' review into the situation at Collingwood made this explicit: 'What is clear is that racism at the club has resulted in profound and enduring harm to First Nations and African players. The racism affected them, their communities, and set dangerous norms for the public'.[3]

Racism, fear, indignity and the harm these carry, all infect our community standards. If they are tolerated and accepted, they become part of our culture and everyone learns 'that's the way things roll around here'. Reflection is discouraged. It becomes too confronting to acknowledge bias and privilege. Besides, it couldn't be true, right, because I'm not a racist. And so we tell ourselves false narratives as a way of avoiding reality and our own responsibility to help change things. Could there be anything more disrespectful than denying a person's lived experience while you enjoy the benefits and privileges stemming, however indirectly, from their treatment? The impact of this defies precise measurement, but we know some things about the consequences: Life feels oppressive. Trauma is relived. Lives are lost, and opportunities and human potential are forgone. Families and communities are destroyed. The hypocrisy in our pride over small steps of progress is shown up. We ignore the truth and the indignity of what someone has had to endure because of the convenience of looking the other way.

'Too often the [club's] reaction was defensive rather than proactive and this aggravated, rather than mitigated, the impact of that racism on the people who experienced it', the 'Do Better' review found.[4] This is familiar territory. It often seems to be how the story unfolds, whether we are looking at cases of racism, sexual harassment or other inconvenient truths.

In Australia, we love our sports heroes because they are who we want to be. Similarly, we indulge a vision of our sporting clubs as paragons—we like to think they are as pure and as uncomplicated as our furious love and our hopes for their sustained success. Our footy clubs in particular have become our churches. They are one of the few public institutions that are growing in membership, and many feel deeply invested, financially and psychologically, in the quest for wins. And so in the face of unpalatable revelations—such as when the Brazilian-born Lumumba was nicknamed 'Chimp' by a number of his Collingwood teammates—we turn on ourselves, engaging in self-denial, too quick to forgive and to resist demanding accountability.

We nod knowingly when leaders dismiss allegations of racism by implying the victim has some form of mental health issue: 'I know he's had a tough time recently. I hope he's doing okay.' Yes, we get it. Instead of listening and engaging, instead of suspending your own privilege for a moment to think about what it's like to be the other, we all hear what you are saying. It is immodestly dressed up in polite code, but we hear it nevertheless. You are saying: 'They are completely nuts and you shouldn't believe anything they say and we should all be focused on winning the grand final this year.'

'Phew,' everyone thinks. Awkward moment over. The implication that someone is unhinged is a tool oft-used to undermine a victim. Attack their credibility and then you do not have to deal with the allegation, much less the substantive issues. When someone bravely puts up their hand and asserts that they have been a victim of racism, they usually do not do it thinking it's going to enhance their career; they do it knowing that it's likely to levy a significant personal and professional cost. And they are usually right about this.

Anyone who has observed an unfolding workplace or public sexual harassment crisis will understand how potent it is to imply that a person is 'unwell' or has some 'wellbeing issues'—it is a subtle but powerful shield against uncomfortable admissions. Of course, this is not to say that every single allegation anyone ever makes is true. But the truth becomes even more elusive when confronted by a fundamental strategy of disrespect, an approach that makes it seem reasonable, if not safe, for people to join the 'I don't believe her' group. It prevents significant consideration of, or regard for, another person's rights. It pushes that person's experience out of thought and visibility. And this should matter to us. Not only are we letting people who should be held accountable off the hook, we are also excusing ourselves from taking responsibility, aiding and abetting false alibis, lowering our norms and limiting our connections as human beings. This is why respect matters.

In late 2018, federal member of parliament Julia Banks made what must have been an agonising decision to quit the Liberal Party and join the crossbench, citing the bullying behaviour of some of her political peers. Banks was a respected MP who had entered parliament with an impressive legal work history, winning the marginal Victorian seat of Chisholm off the Labor Party in the 2016 federal election—the only Coalition candidate to snatch a seat from the Opposition. In the wake of her resignation, she probably knew that her prospects of re-election as an independent were slim. Indeed, in the 2019 national election she unsuccessfully contested the Victorian seat of Flinders, which was won by federal Health and Aged Care Minister Greg Hunt. Her earlier allegations about a culture of intimidation and vindictiveness in the Commonwealth Parliament, on both sides of the aisle, had proven unwelcome and, despite corroboration by many others, they had been dismissed. The low point came on 27 November 2018 when Banks began talking about how women were being treated in parliament, and five male Liberal MPs literally turned their backs to her. This could be interpreted as nothing other than an act of disrespect.

At the time of Julia Bank's resignation, Prime Minister Morrison said that his first concern was for her 'welfare and wellbeing', adding that he was 'giving her every comfort and support'.[5] Did you get the message, the not-so-subtle one? The implication was that Banks was mentally injured, unwell, that she was probably making all of this up. The subtext here was 'Not to be believed'. It's a tactic that is used time and time again, a tactic that is part of the social playbook, and to some extent has been institutionalised in politics, sport, media and the law. What was needed was a respectful acknowledgement of Julia Banks' experiences, not a dehumanising denial of them.

DEEP WATER

In recent times, watching the rights and credibility of victims of harassment, discrimination and rape being attacked in the Australian Parliament has served as a life-sapping reminder that any belief in progress on equality and the elimination of sexism is misconceived, a mirage.

In February 2021, when Prime Minister Scott Morrison stood up in parliament to address questions about the alleged mid-2019 rape of Brittany Higgins in the office of then defence industry minister Linda Reynolds, my disrespect antennae were already wobbling.[6] The Prime Minister had earlier sought to distance himself from this accusation of a serious crime in the fulcrum of politics and law, the Commonwealth Parliament. But after his initial dismissiveness and an attempt to wave through the public revelation of Higgins' story—'Move on, nothing new to see here!'—the Prime Minister got snagged on the threat of a public outcry and some quickfire fact-checking. The emerging information raised even more questions, along with suggestions of a cover-up and a strong sense of how her Liberal minders had abandoned Brittany Higgins—and many others, as it turns out. I suspect Morrison realised then that, on this issue, he was in very deep water, which has only become deeper as the stories of other victims and their private pain have made their way into the public domain.

The day after the Prime Minister's tin-ear dismissal of the allegations, he tried to show some empathy by sharing with the public a discussion he had had with his wife and reflecting on how he would want his daughters to be treated. Some were confused as to why this was the subject of a good deal of outrage. It is because it implies that women only deserve respect if they are attached to someone—read 'a man'. It suggests that only in the context of their relationship as a daughter or a wife should a woman's rights be acknowledged and upheld—women seemingly do not have any agency independent of who they are married to or their status as a daughter.

The Prime Minister's remarks showcased for many how his instincts on this issue fell well short of widespread expectations about how to express our collective shock and revulsion at the claims we were hearing. Leaders must help us process any confronting information that is put before us. That is what we look for in their responses. But in this case, the response was a bitterly disappointing one. The Prime Minister not only took too long to reflect and display empathy for Brittany Higgins, he had to be nudged into doing it. And by the politics of the situation, of all things.

The chilling history set out in the final report of the Royal Commission into Institutional Responses to Child Sexual Abuse in December 2017 reset the threshold of intolerance for victim shaming.[7] Decades of denial and institutional cover-ups, recognisable by the many who directly experienced this horror and by the people who loved them, have built greater expectations about the acknowledgement of abuse—this was all just too familiar to victims and those who know the truth they speak. There is now a heightened scrutiny and awareness of the pincer movements of institutional denial, and its often irreversible harm and consequences. The dehumanising repudiations that victims are subjected to when their experiences are treated like a political hot potato remind them they have nothing to lose. The worst things one can imagine have already happened to them—except that victims say they often feel violated all over again by the 'system'.

As more and more gut-wrenching details of Brittany Higgins' accusations were revealed, much of the public coverage turned into a morass of who knew and did what to whom and when. The particulars of text messages, voicemails, the involvement of security guards and the federal police, all just came tumbling out. What made this even more horrifying was that much of the new information was also new to Brittany Higgins— things she had not been told, facts that she had been denied, about her. The management of a political scandal had clearly taken priority over the victim's interests. We should resist the cynical temptation to drolly dismiss this as a 'And you're surprised about that?' moment. We should be outraged.

We should remember that these allegations involve a serious crime, one committed against a young ministerial staffer. It was a crime against all of us. Where was the instinctive respect for Brittany Higgins, for her rights? Imagine the most awful thing happening to you and then having it play out across the political arena.

My own first reaction was to think about how extraordinarily brave Higgins was in voicing what had happened, followed by concern about her welfare but also her future self, as this will now be an indelible part of what is documented about her life. We must all remember that we have an obligation to respect and support her beyond the short span of the media–political cycle. We must not just let the dogs bark and the caravan roll on. We must not.

The Victorian Parliament was sitting the week this all became public. Many of my female colleagues began sharing whispered stories about their own experiences in Canberra. A lot of MPs and staff members have worked in the 'Canberra bubble' in previous lives and there was a strong tone of 'There but for the grace of God go I'—these allegations summoned memories of the occasions when the victim could just as easily have been them. However, the empathy and horror exhibited by many of my colleagues was not only due to an awareness of possible sliding door moments. They were angered and outraged by how, despite the universal rhetoric of respect for women, many knew but did nothing. Many misled, lied, failed to disclose important information, with the alleged rape of a young woman politely shepherded out the door while government talking points of the day were repeated in the background.

Let me make this simple. Rebuilding respect in public institutions means you should not attempt to cover up a rape. You should not ignore or 'manage away' the victim. 'Brittany,' the PM kept saying, rather than 'Brittany Higgins' or 'Ms Higgins,' presenting a familiarity, an intimacy, that was simply not real, disrespectfully not using her full name. As Jacqueline Maley wrote in the Fairfax newspapers on 21 February 2021:

> It may not have been deliberate, but the persistent use of Higgins' first name, and Morrison's comments about consulting his wife Jenny on how to handle the alleged rape, all gave the impression that this was a matter to do with Women's Feelings. Women's Feelings is a private emotional realm, tricky to navigate and best left to the ladies. It has little to do with male leaders, and nothing to do with important matters of state.

In other words, rape is women's business.

The Prime Minister is a smart and successful politician. As the political quicksand of sexual abuse around his government deepened, the government tried to find more secure land on which to defend itself amidst a growing perception of a cover-up. But in the political and media worlds, noses are finely tuned to the scent of displaced responsibility.

The uncomfortably violent colloquialism used to describe one colleague shifting the blame to another refers to being 'thrown under a bus'. It certainly seemed as if the Prime Minister was very keen to draw a sharp distinction between his own knowledge and accountability and that of his Defence Minister, Linda Reynolds, as well as that of other ministerial colleagues who, it was later revealed, had some knowledge of these events. Many staff who worked across numerous offices, including that of the Prime Minister, apparently knew about what had happened, as did security guards at Parliament House and some members of the Australian Federal Police, yet the Prime Minister seemingly did not. It would appear that awareness and responsibility do not extend to the highest office in the land.

Whether you love them or hate them, you should expect your political leaders to be much better teachers when it comes to respect. As an MP myself, I am conscious that we are the stewards of important institutions that bolster civil stability and the rule of law, and act as a bulwark against the excesses of power. I also know that showing the necessary respect to these institutions does not mean protecting them, or those who inhabit them, from change. I hope it does not come as a surprise to hear that those inhabitants are not perfect. Far from it—we come with many limitations. We make mistakes. We fail. We are very human. But we need to be more humane. We need to stop looking around at the bin fires that masquerade as 'public debate' and rather reflect on our own contributions to the degeneration of civil discussion.

Rosie Batty, the 2015 Australian of the Year, is a passionate domestic violence campaigner. She is also a survivor of the most unspeakable crime: the murder of her eleven-year-old son Luke by his father in February 2014 in the Victorian township of Tyabb. At significant personal cost, and despite her profound grief, she began campaigning for structural and legal change to prevent family violence, and she has not stopped. Batty played a key role in the establishment in Victoria in early 2015 of the Royal Commission into Family Violence, which was rightfully seen as a watershed moment—a once-in-a-lifetime opportunity to drive changes to domestic violence prevention, funding and policing models; the management of risks; secure accommodation and ongoing safety; and specialist legal responses.[8]

All states and territories have endured elections where a frenzied 'law and order' campaign takes off, accompanied by a lot of fearmongering but not a lot of facts, such as that the number-one risk to most women and children is the violence they are subjected to behind closed doors at home. The Victorian Government's commitment to the Royal Commission into Family Violence reframed the prevention of violence as a mainstream law and order issue, which in turn impacted the attention it received as a policy issue, and the related media coverage, resource allocation and priorities for ongoing reform. This showed respect for the lives of women and children. It told us that the injuring and deaths of family members could no longer be dismissed as 'A domestic gone bad'. It clearly indicated that our system had failed too many times, and that we desperately needed change.

As a prelude to the tabling of the royal commission's final report on 29 March 2016, some survivors of family violence addressed a sitting of the Parliament of Victoria. All of the speakers spoke movingly and beautifully—it was both gut-wrenching and a great honour to hear their stories. I do not underestimate the cost of retraumatisation that advocates pay when standing up to argue for long-overdue reform. These people had come to educate us and make the case for change. Afterwards, the MPs in attendance gave a standing ovation, out of respect for those who had just given something special to parliament, out of respect for the work Rosie Batty had done, and out of respect for her son. All except one, a lone refusal to stand that represented a rejection of Batty and others' exhortations to focus on the real law and order challenge of our time. It was a display of disrespect to those who had shared their pain and hopes for reform. And it became a collective embarrassment—his disrespect became our disrespect. It sent the message that the parliamentary chamber was a place where you could disrespect a woman whose son had been murdered.

The member in question, Graham Watt, was never really forgiven for this. The incident was regularly raised in parliamentary debates, and he was ultimately defeated at the next state election in 2018.

One of the key findings of the Royal Commission into Family Violence was that gender inequality is a key driver of violence against women. Building respect for women is crucial in the effort to eliminate the structural causes of this inequality. Demonstrating disrespect for women has all sorts of awful consequences—the impact of public displays of this behaviour is bigger than the sum of all of the parts. It creates a safe space for the shaming, blaming and ultimately the dehumanisation of women. It creates a culture of acceptance of this. It disempowers women, exposes us to indignity, hampers our ability to genuinely enjoy a life of full equality. The rate of women being murdered by people they know, and perhaps love or once loved, is a pretty compelling reason to do something about this, I would have thought.

DISRESPECTING THE EXPERTS

The era of COVID-19 has served up a raft of examples of how our declining trust in institutions of knowledge, and expertise in general, has led to a lack of respect for science. For example, over in the United States last year, we saw the supposed leader of the free world, (now former) president Donald Trump, issue pronouncements about the cause, source and treatment of COVID-19 that directly harmed the people who took his advice. There are legitimate debates and many unknowns concerning the spread of, and the response to, COVID-19. But across the world, there is also an incontrovertible medical consensus on basic infection-prevention strategies. Of course, 2020 was the year of a US election, and so something as self-evidently nonsensical as refusing to wear a mask in public became a symbol for the diminishing influence of and respect for independent expertise. The phrase 'alternative facts' became part of the political parlance; inconvenient facts were dismissed as fake news.

Pandemics are not just health emergencies. They are also communication emergencies. In such a situation, it is essential that governments, health services and the media can rapidly relay facts and credible advice to all communities, in an easily comprehensible format. And so it is critical that communities, and self-evidently the individuals that comprise them, trust and respect the accuracy and the urgency of that information. Respect for expertise can either save or cost human lives; it can promote or destroy economic and social wellbeing. The behaviour of a few can determine the outcome for many.

It is in all our interests that false information is quickly identified and called out, so that quackery and falsehoods do not gain traction. Part of a respect for science and the considered opinions of experts is accepting that interventions have both a collective and an individual impact. The respect we show is not just for knowledge but for others in our community too, highlighting our responsibility to each other.

The spectacularly self-indulgent behaviour of, among others, the woman who in November 2020 argued with staff in a Melbourne Bunnings outlet over the requirement to wear a mask, apparently claiming it was an imposition on her sovereign rights, politicised this simple, effective action.[9] I often wondered during the mask disobedience epidemic what it would it take for people to just accept the science and take action to help stop the spread of the virus. Compliance became a proxy for other disputes, but it really does not indicate whether you are for or against the government that holds power in your city, state or country. Freedoms—including freedom of speech—are always bumping into each other, even conflicting. Rights and responsibilities sometimes have to be reconciled, or one privileged over another. There are always tough policy calls that government at all levels has had to debate and work through. The quality of the evidence is what ultimately matters, especially when difficult decisions have to be made.

The rise and continuing influence of the anti-vaccination movement provides a good example of why it is important to nurture respect for expertise. Highly organised and determined, this movement spreads lies to frighten people. It champions discredited information to try and woo the vaccine-hesitant, making it dangerous in the best of times. Its efforts have been made easier by how the more recent challenges of COVID-19 have at times obscured the heartening history of the benefits that vaccinations have bestowed on public health.

As the Victorian minister for health, I learned how deadly even a small outbreak of pertussis (whooping cough) can be. I will never forget an intensive care nurse describing to me the horrors of caring for an infant who had turned blue around the mouth, heaving breaths in and out of their small body, their traumatised parents looking on. This experience was made all the more frustrating because, as with measles, which itself can have serious consequences, pertussis is a vaccine-preventable disease. Some people are unable to be vaccinated due to, for example, a compromised immune system, or their age. This makes it urgent that we strive for a community-wide 95 per cent vaccination rate. Such a level of immunisation may deliver herd immunity, a cute-sounding term that basically means that when a significant proportion of the population is vaccinated, they can provide some protection for those who have not yet achieved that immunity. Above all, promoting respect for sources of truth—in this case registered, regulated and qualified medical professionals—is essential as we seek to vaccinate the globe against COVID-19 and its variants. There is still a lot to learn about the virus, but the threshold issues concerning the vaccination program in Australia are well resolved. The jury is not out.

As a parliamentarian, I was involved in law reform that required Victorian children to be vaccinated in order to attend early-childhood services, unless they had a medical reason not to be. This reform, which was introduced at the beginning of 2016, did not acknowledge or accept a conscientious objection as grounds for an exemption.

The science in support of vaccination is not a matter of conscience. The time of enrolment in kindergarten and child care was a great opportunity to identify children who had not been vaccinated or who had missed a vaccination, and to work with their families to organise an inoculation. It was also a chance to engage with anyone who may have been persuaded by any of the multiple sources of misinformation and conspiracy theories online, connecting them with maternal child health nurses and general practitioners.

Predictably, the announcement of this reform made the anti-vaxxers apoplectic. Of all the organised political forces I have been exposed to—and there have been many, believe me—the anti-vaxxers have been the most vicious and threatening as a collective. Other groups taking part in bioethical and social policy debates have held their views in opposition to mine very passionately, but none are in the same league. Some of the efforts against vaccination were standard—mass email campaigns are not unusual as a source of advocacy. However, the emails I received were often vile and explicitly threatening, including wishing terminal illnesses and attacks upon my children. The online attacks, some of which countenanced criminal acts, were also deeply sexist. The staff at the offices where I worked who were required to answer the phones were also often subjected to such behaviour, similarly at a scale they would never before have encountered—not even the seasoned political staffers.

The anti-vaxxers often taped their abuse and deposited it online as some form of trophy, and on some days the phones simply had to be turned off, such was the relentlessness of the abuse. But then the visitors began arriving. Perhaps unwisely, they sometimes filmed themselves trying to enter offices and reception areas that were closed to them. I remember an incident that occurred at one of my annual 'welcoming the babies' ceremonies, which was really a fun way to celebrate new mums and their babies in my electorate by putting on a morning tea and connecting people with local groups and services. It was also a magnificent opportunity to meet and cuddle a lot of gorgeous babies. Yes, I know, politicians and babies, such a cliché. Well, you can imagine my horror as we became aware that an attempt was being made by some anti-vaxxer parents to disrupt the event. I was very concerned about the risks of unvaccinated children being brought to a gathering of newborns as a form of protest, but some deft screening by my staff resulted in a swift resolution—and some predictable forms of abuse.

Putting fear into the parents of newborn babies was an odious stock-in-trade for these groups. But their endeavours also included graffitiing the posters in clinics and hospitals that reminded people to vaccinate their children or to update their own inoculations. Some activists would proudly post photographs online of their graffiti work on the backs of toilet doors in some of Melbourne's specialist maternity hospitals. Of course they did, these being the ideal places to generate disrespect for science and distrust in health professionals. For people who have just had a baby, confidence in their own parenting judgement has its rough days. Running a campaign to try and persuade new parents that health professionals are intent on trying to get you to poison your own baby because they are slaves to the pharmaceutical industry is a special kind of low in my book. An anti-vaxxer with a Sharpie in their hand can do untold damage to the health and wellbeing of many. You have been warned.

In contrast to the disrespect shown to science and communal responsibility that I came to know all too well as the health minister, I also met many people who were committed to sticking up for the facts. I am still grateful for how these people, mainly health professionals, were so devoted to addressing misinformation in the public domain. Doctors, paramedics, nurses, midwives and allied health staff work diligently every day to prevent and treat illnesses, and for many, ongoing exposure to the incidence of vaccine-preventable diseases is a source of intense frustration. A number of these professionals fought the good fight online in the face of the anti-vaxxer onslaughts. Taking up this fight came with consequences: abusive calls to their clinics, vexatious reports to professional bodies and online hurt was the cost of defending the facts, science and good health. Fortunately, while I know that respect for the media—just as for my chosen profession—is not at an all-time high, on the issue of vaccination, my experience with news outlets and journalists was generally very good. We seemed to reach an unspoken consensus not to let the quackery run riot. Important in this was using the experts to help explain the facts— the community has a high level of trust in health professionals, and consequently they are terrific ambassadors for the truth, especially when it comes to health care.

One devoted doctor monitored the online snarks and threats of some of the anti-vaccination leaders, very kindly alerting me to any brags online about disturbing my offices or other threats. Many of the planned intimidations were reported to the police. Some attempts were diverted. Sometimes we got just enough warning from our 'friends of science' to get the office physically closed and the staff prepared. Sometimes scuffles and police or security involvement ensued.

I had to become very cautious about announcing or tweeting my presence at community events, which for a politician, to be frank, is a little awkward. A couple of anti-vaxxer devotees would track my whereabouts and issue a call to arms if, for example, I was at the opening of a local playground. I became adept at simultaneously detecting the stride of an anti-vaxxer as they marched across an oval in my direction, and scoping my surroundings for potential escape routes. I might have found their fervour admirable if it was not so dangerous.

My children on the whole paid a more modest price. They would return from outings or sporting events and report someone making rather colourful anti-vaccination comments to them to pass on to me. Much to their chagrin, these experiences meant I would not allow them to have access to social media accounts. Yes, in many ways it was a convenient excuse. However, the viciousness of the attacks I experienced, with the wellbeing of my children invoked in the vitriol, made it pretty obvious to me that my kids could not enjoy the thrills and spills of the digital world without being targeted by or otherwise exposed to this ugly underbelly.

Reason and respect is desperately needed in debates that literally can cost lives. That said, pretending that a comprehensively scientifically discredited viewpoint has equal standing or legitimacy in such a debate is plain wrong; we must not provide a platform to those who are propagating totally debunked myths. There is often some type of dispute or disagreement in the initial phase of coming to grips with an issue. However, evidence and time will eventually build a comprehensive consensus on matters that have been widely researched, contested, scrutinised, reviewed and debated. The voices of scientific authority must be cultivated in order to reach this tipping point.

No one field of expertise ought to be beyond question. But let us not pretend that this is like a modern-day game of pass the parcel, where each person, side or argument gets a turn. Not all sides are equal in some debates. The practice of shouting over or undermining credible proof must not be allowed to dominate our policy debates. We must always allow for and assess disconfirming evidence, but the theories and arguments we know to be simply wrong or even dangerous should be treated as such.

I have shared this story of my war with the anti-vaccination crowd to show how deep the fissures can run when it comes to showing respect for science and expertise. I did not expect this when I became a proponent of something as simple as encouraging people to vaccinate their children. In Australia, we may consider the political circus that unfolded in the United States in 2020 with a degree of smug derision—I too shook my head and became almost immune to the shock and awe of US politics. But there is much for us to learn from what happened across the Pacific. For one thing, it is well worth trying to better understand why so many patent falsehoods about COVID-19 were genuinely believed by so many Americans, sometimes almost rapturously so.

The politics of mask-wearing will no doubt continue to be a source of social, political, medical and corporate discussion. Arguably more damaging was the public disrespect shown to medical experts by the American Republican leadership. For example, think back to when Trump implied that the political preferences of Anthony Fauci, at the time the director of the White House Coronavirus Task Force, meant that the doctor's medical advice was compromised. The president then further undermined the credibility of the advice being issued by the task force by asserting that Dr Fauci had 'made a lot of mistakes'. I'm sure he had. What Trump was seeking to do, however, was not to hold Fauci to account for any substantial failings in his post, but simply to undermine Fauci's authority because he did not say what Trump wanted him to say. The president implied that the doctor was not to be trusted—'Don't believe that guy.' I am loathe to draw attention to any of the former US president's tweets, but it is worth mentioning that Trump also retweeted some social media with #FireFauci as one of his calling-card hashtags. Can you imagine Prime Minister Morrison retweeting something sassy that ended with #FireMurphy, or NSW Premier Gladys Berejiklian sharing a social media post with #FireChant? Thankfully, this is unthinkable.

As contested as some of Australia's COVID-19 restrictions have been, there has been a good level of respect for the motivations, experience and expertise of the health and medical officers advising our Commonwealth and state governments and territories. Yes, there have been debates about differing risk appetites, the quality of infection-prevention responses, and concerns about where the burdens of this pandemic have fallen. Nonetheless, what remained despite these frustrations was a basic respect for the advice of our health professionals.

The COVID-19 pandemic has revealed weaknesses in our social and political systems. It has also highlighted how stark inequality made our response to the pandemic imperfect due to the social and economic realities of how many people live and work. Again, people arguing against the consensus health advice sometimes made things very challenging, and there were protests, although the levels of support and participation regarding these were relatively low. People expressed their frustration and grief in different ways, and for those who have lost loved ones during this time, their need for understanding and accountability goes on. Still, we did not let our frustration overwhelm our respect for the clinical advice we were being given, and for those who were giving it.

After all, the health professionals guiding us through these uncharted and potentially deadly waters have also been at the forefront of risk and exposure—staffing health services in all their forms has meant carrying the risk of infection. Our communities have also been supported, if not held together, by the administrative, enforcement, transport and retail staff who have subjected themselves and their families to personal risk. I hope the experience of how fleeting normality can be and the new awareness of our reliance on these services also increase how much we value these workforces. I suspect there is still much we can do to show respect to these workers—fair pay, secure and safe work, and an acknowledgement of how critical these people are to a decent way of life, these would be a good way of demonstrating this.

As a general rule, when we needed to be told some direct truths about the virulence and impact of this virus, we respected those who had to deliver these unwelcome messages. Perhaps watching the horrendous scenes taking place internationally reminded us of our own vulnerability, and so despite the mistrust of politicians in this country, there was gratitude for the relentlessness of their work—albeit with responses varying from begrudging acknowledgement to enthusiastic cheerleading. In Victoria, I witnessed this work up close, and I cannot overstate how demanding the required leadership was, and how devoted Premier Andrews was to these responsibilities, in ways that were not always publicly visible. People of different political persuasions (granted, not all) made the point that while they disagreed with some of the state government's decisions, they respected the Premier's commitment to the state and to the constancy of leadership. I suspect that is the case for the leaders of the other states and territories as well.

VIRTUAL AGREEMENT

We are all capable of respecting those with whom we disagree. We can do this when talking about politics. We can sit next to supporters of the opposition at the footy and other sports matches. We can argue the toss about our favourite foods: how to cook them, how to eat them, what to call them. (A light-hearted aside in case you are wondering: I sit on the potato cake side of the potato cake versus scallop debate, because a scallop is a form of shellfish, but I can respect the fact that South Australians have a different point of view.) We do need to acknowledge respect to cultivate it. We need to demonstrate it. In fact, we need to honour it wherever and whenever it is shown. On the flip side, we need to resist the temptation to dismiss it as an old-fashioned exhortation to make children feel bad about themselves.

Respect matters because it helps us to take on board other perspectives. Insight enhances our understanding and awareness, which in turn drives better decision-making and behaviours. The dismissal of another point of view can plant the seeds for the dismissal of another person, which is the road to conflict and cruelty. Being adamant can insulate us from taking responsibility for the impact of our judgements. We can be better than that.

The digital world has presented us with all sorts of wonderful opportunities when it comes to sharing views—and a lot of problems we do not seem to be able to solve. Some of these problems are regulatory and some are cultural. The sheer pace of technological discovery and evolution, the intimidating potential of big data and artificial intelligence, make it feel like the infinite is unknowable. But the existing structures of state sovereignty make this world very difficult to regulate. Nudges are often tried, with modest impacts. Public affairs diplomacy, financial and procurement incentives, or just begging digital barons to behave—these are tried and tired responses. As for the costs, electoral interference, dark web activity, fake news and scams are the all-too-familiar reflections of technology's downside.

There is no avoiding the digital, though. The reality is that much of our political and civic life is curated if not conducted online, or it soon will be. The reliance on data, for one thing, is a long-accepted essential tool for political parties to win elections. Politics is no different to the commercial, media and entertainment worlds—to the extent that any of those are still separate spheres—where most of us already feel left behind in our attempts at adjustment, no matter how digitally woke our posturing is. In everything from education to parenting, we are all scurrying to be impactful and relevant. There is, however, a deeper sense that we are in a black hole of sorts, ungrounded and unprepared. It should not, therefore, have come as any great shock to learn that digital platforms can be adept at showcasing the ugly side of human beings when it comes to political and public debates.

Providing a practically limitless forum for
people to offer views and share ideas, or links to
ideas, in and of itself can have democratising senti-
ments. 'The world is now flat,' some cried out in the
early days of their digital forays, besotted by new-
found opportunities for expression, delighting in
how their voices could be heard unfettered by the
structures of government and media permission.
One benefit has been the potential for political
organisation and change, for evoking government
accountability, that has been witnessed in periods
of uprising such as the Arab Spring—the relatively brief period in 2010–11 when the Middle
East became a crucible of public protest. Overall,
human rights group are now better able to
monitor those who are at risk of abuse or oppres-
sion, or of simply disappearing, because of their
activism. No-one requires permission to speak,
albeit the channels for doing so are not always
open. However, groups devoted to terror and
war in all of their manifestations are also availing
themselves of the digital opportunities to pursue
their agendas.

And it is difficult to identify reliable sources of insightful debate and trustworthy analysis in the online world—or if you will, 'facts' or 'truth'. Lies, rumours and mistruths are easily propagated. No-one wants to miss out on new information, however fabricated it might be; indeed, everyone wants to be the first to share it. 'Huge if true!' labels are attached to many social media shares. Once false assertions are widely distributed, it almost becomes irrelevant that the information is wrong—the more it is shared, the more 'truthiness' it assumes. This a challenge for how modern media works and how it will sustain itself commercially in the future. It is a life-threatening problem in areas of the world beset by civil conflict and lawless-ness, where false information can fire up violent conflicts and persecution.

What is it about the online world that makes it easy for us to lose respect for facts and truth there? What is it about this environment that can make us be dismissive of the rights and dignity of other human beings, content to be bystanders to their public maulings? Why do we tolerate the extremes of abuse some inflict, as if it is merely a valid expression of their rage at a changing world?

The racism and sexism that hurts and harms so many people online is a strident act of disrespect. I often wonder if we have always been like this and online platforms have simply enabled racists and misogynists to connect with and embolden each other. I wonder if the anonymity afforded to the keyboard warrior is the cause of these issues or simply facilitates the real problems. I recall the homophobic diatribes, so vicious and hurtful, in the law-reform debates of recent times, so frightening in their rejection of the humanity, rights and dignity of the lesbian, gay, bisexual, transgender, intersex, queer (or questioning) community. What is the source of such hatred?

There are, of course, many fantastic and ongoing displays of collaboration, inquiry, connection, caring and view-sharing on the internet. But the extremism of the online ugliness demonstrates that we have not yet developed mature social and cultural mores about how to engage with each other civilly online. Yes, we plan and deliver curriculums for children on cyber safety. We run anti-bullying classes. We teach our kids how to conduct respectful relationships and encourage healthier attitudes. But young people then get the polar opposite world view simply by seeing how many adults engage in digital abuse, spreading hatred and disrespect, unbothered by the consequences.

I have been horrified, both as a parent and as a public representative, at the abuse some parents publish on social media sites that is aimed at teachers at their kids' schools. I am not talking about one-off lapses, someone reacting to having a hard day, but sustained, targeted invective and cyberbullying. Many teachers and school principals have shared with me the professional and emotional costs of being a victim of this disrespect. The fastest-growing area of workers' compensation claims in education settings—and likely in most professional settings—is that of mental injury. And children are experts when it comes to identifying this hypocrisy. How can we develop, teach, set and enforce expectations around respectful online behaviour for young people when so many of the adults around them proudly share their digital dogfights? Having the courage of your convictions or being an outlier regarding your view in a debate—or supporting the dominant view, for that matter—is not an excuse to behave in a disrespectful way. Nor can this lack of respect be justified by claiming provocation; that is an inadequate response.

Abuse is also a significant issue for members of parliament. When you put yourself forward for public office, you expect some crushing criticism. The nature of politics is defined by different visions of our community, and differing opinions about the social, political and economic architecture necessary to achieve a vision. People have been yelling at each other about such matters since the day dot. But the arrival of new digital platforms has opened the door to greater carelessness about the impact of our actions on others, to the demonisation of whole categories of people, to the desire to publicly hurt someone so badly that the piercing insults and imagined humiliation become more important than the argument you first sought to make. Anything goes, apparently, which completely undermines our ability to successfully talk through complicated topics.

The uncomplicated topics are being contaminated by hatred as well. The harm endured by the LGBTIQ community during the marriage-equality debate in the lead-up to the legalisation of same-sex marriage in December 2017—not just the homophobia but the fundamental denial of humanity—was undoubtedly made even more unbearable due to the horrific attacks being posted online. Respect means having due regard for a person's rights, feelings and wishes. Why would you not want to show that, even if you hold a view very passionately?

Equipped with a keyboard, some people behave like monsters. Is it because they are monsters? Or is it just because they can behave in this way without being identified and taken to task? There is a spectrum of egregious and moronic online behaviour. It may be tempting to always conflate the assertions of someone with whom we disagree with stupidity or a sociopathology. But be wary of projection.

There are lines that should not be crossed when it comes to online behaviour, although sometimes they are thick and sometimes indistinct. There is certainly a broad consensus when it comes to vilification. However imperfect and in need of reform some might be, there are anti-vilification laws in play all over Australia, in jurisdictions with different political leaderships. Competing notions of protection against discrimination and vilification and limits to freedom of speech in the main have been reconciled, sometimes via the pragmatic tool of political negotiation to secure a majority (usually in an upper house) to get legislation through parliament. This is a good thing, as most laws help drive positive social norms and behaviours. However, our limited ability to regulate the internet means that there has been little success in using anti-vilification laws to persuade the harbingers of hate that their bad behaviour has legal consequences, much less hold people accountable for their actions online. It is unfortunate, because these laws could be used as a sharp tool to create more respectful debates.

Several parliaments have been grappling with how to regulate and enforce better responses to these complicated issues, with vilification edging closer to constituting a breach of criminal laws. But tougher laws and more effective enforcement alone will not help us rebuild a culture of respect online, not as long as the bullying, vilification and online games of 'stacks on' continue in any form. People ought to be able to participate in digital life without jeopardising their mental health, but we remain a long way from that. This means that good people will continue to be driven from public life by racism, misogyny, homophobia and xenophobia—for some, it becomes so awful that they feel they can no longer work for the rest of the community, be they journalists, politicians, teachers or others.

'Block and ignore,' people are advised. And I know many who attempt this. But if an important part of your job is communicating with the public, this is simply unsustainable. Rage inevitably fuels more rage and creates a self-fulfilling climate of hate. 'Twitter is just an echo chamber,' we all scream at each other in the echo chamber. Those who endure being abused do so at great personal cost. I have witnessed first-hand what can happen when you are the victim of hate speech; the emotional consequences of having your race, your cultural identity, your sexuality, your looks, your family attacked; the fallout when the available responses to such attacks are limited and ineffective.

All spheres of public life need great diversity, to better represent the communities that public figures serve. Diversity means bringing greater experience and different voices to the table. It generates more insights into the ways of the world, how markets work, what communities want, what the future might hold. Better, more informed debates can then occur, and better decisions can then be made, whether they concern performance, profitability or principle. However, we need to ensure that these environments are respectful ones. My fear is that many people who would make a terrific contribution to, say, politics are simply not willing to subject themselves and their families to the kind of abuse hurled in that world on a regular basis.

Female members of parliament, just like female journalists and other professional women, are entitled to feel weary about the sexist abuse they are often subjected to online. This can range from claptrap about what women look like to threats of sexual violence and death. Emailing a member of parliament so that you can detail the violent criminal acts you wish to subject her to, as well as giving her some feedback on how she should wear her hair, takes a special kind of misogynist. The situation is significantly worse for those women whose cultural background or sexuality— perceived or real—is also attacked. My experience of enforcement and security services is that they take the criminal threats seriously. However, the elusiveness of the perpetrators, mainly because of their online anonymity, means many investigations are unable to proceed very far. In how many other workplace environments would behaviour that veers from disrespect to outright criminal illegality be tolerated? Yet we are told to ignore it, to block it, and it will all go away.

Once upon a time I would have been called

Ms Hennessy. These days customer service people begin conversations with 'Hi, is it OK if I call you Jill?' Sometimes I want to say, 'No it's not OK to call me Jill.' But now no-one wants to look like a cranky Karen. Yet I listened to how Prime Minister Morrison referred to Brittany Higgins and, like so many women, I felt offended on Ms Higgins' behalf. In using her first name, he was being overly familiar, subtly diminishing and downplaying her experience, signalling a lack of respect. We now accept a level of informality and familiarity that conflates and confuses the difference between the personal and the public, the private and the profes- sional. Which brings us back to the transformation of the public square by the emergence of social media. This almost entirely unregulated space affords anonymity and the unfettered venting of ill-informed views, misogyny and misanthropy. Under such a cloak of invisibility, it seems that the inhibitions that underpin civility are tossed aside. So the disempowered, the disenfranchised and the disengaged are free to abuse and bully, and shut down opinions they do not share. Social media is

JILL HENNESSY

a space in which disrespect now flourishes freely. Disrespect has become commonplace as the way in which we make ourselves heard above the din of other angry voices. And this ubiquitous disrespect in public discourse has led to disrespect in the workplace, on the sports field, in parliamentary politics, in our courts, between men and women. Without respect, the ties that bind us, that make us a community, will fray. Instead, we need them to be stronger, as they always are when we reassert the need for respect, for courtesy, for kindness, for empathy.

ANTICIPATING TRAUMA

There is concern among many women in public life that raising issues such as those I have just described may be interpreted as them being weak and whiny. We are often trying to stave off the suggestion that women 'can't hack it'. This sexist stereotype is a persistent one, even if it is now expressed in much more hushed tones than it once was. Yes, this despite what we should have learned from the often highly disrespectful treatment of Julia Gillard after she became Australia's first female prime minister in June 2010, and which she reacted to so memorably in her anti-misogyny speech of October 2012.[10] We are all diminished by this. We all have an interest in ensuring that institutions that are vital to our democracy, our prosperity, our history and our future are not undermined by disrespect. Politics in particular cannot afford to present as even more unattractive to bright, emotionally intelligent, innovative and diverse people whose participation we desperately need to continue to lift us as a nation. So respect matters. And calling out disrespect matters too, including when it is directed at people we disagree with.

Unfortunately, we seem to be in a mode of having to actively prepare ourselves for discussions where we can anticipate trauma with a fairly high degree of certainty. For example, consider recent debates on the banning of gay suppression or conversion 'therapy' and transgender recognition on birth certificates.[11] These brought out such harmful invective that even I was shocked—although many people in the community and the parliament made the point to me that this is the experience of many LQBTIQ people every day. Ironically, I am not sure if the opponents of these changes realised that their abusive behaviour actually made a rather pertinent case for the need for reforms that sought to entrench respect for people's rights and humanity. They embodied the very reason why the state needs to intervene and stop people from being denied the right to be themselves, as well as protecting that right.

Among the vile tactics was the letterboxing in some communities of filthy anonymous flyers that looked like they had been typeset in a back-yard printing press. I remember speaking to the infuriated mother of a seventeen-year-old who had recently come out at his school, and whose mental health and wellbeing was particularly precarious. Imagine how it felt for him, this woman urged me, to have homophobic materials distributed to the homes of his schoolmates and across the local community. She was right to be outraged.

The over-representation of LGBTIQ people in suicide and self-harm statistics places an obligation on us all, though especially on public leaders, to ensure that any debate affecting them is respectful and that there is a swift response to damaging or dangerous contributions. As I have already argued, freedom of speech is not unfettered. Minimising the harm people inflict in policy and political debates is a public interest responsibility of all of us.

Identifying the line between legitimate and respectful debate on one side, and disrespect and harm on the other, will help shape a social consensus. This line will always be contested and a little blurred, and I think we should all accept that. What should not be accepted is the rejection or denial of empathy. We can and should make disrespectful attacks an outlier and build a stronger consensus about our behaviour. I have experienced this capacity to have respectful conversations, even in regard to topics over which there has traditionally been fierce disagreement, and in which much political capital has been invested—debates where there were a lot of competing voices and online debate, but where parliamentarians managed to shepherd the extremist abuse to the periphery without compromising their commitment to the key issues.

The Victorian Parliament decriminalised abortion in 2008, but pro-life groups continue to maintain their opposition to the legislation, expressing this in many ways—some respectful, some not. For as long as I have been a member of the Victorian Parliament, each day that parliament is sitting, a dedicated group of people who are opposed to abortion conduct a quiet protest at the back gate of the building. They have their handwritten signs, and sometimes a fold-up chair, a thermos and an umbrella at hand, even on sunny days—Melbourne's weather is a fickle beast. Some days there will be ten people, some days only two. Whilst I vehemently disagree with their views, I must concede they are very devoted. And of all the times I have walked past them to go to work, I can only recall a single occasion when one of the group overstepped the mark and tried to physically block me from entering the grounds of Parliament

House, calling me a 'baby killer' when I politely declined to take the written material they were thrusting at me. Over the rest of the last decade, we have peacefully coexisted, sharing a reciprocal tired wave in recognition of each other's existence and in a silent concession that neither of us is going to persuade the other of the superiority of their view.

This was not the experience in years past of some patients and staff entering and leaving the health services where abortions are performed. Those opposed to abortion would protest vociferously outside these clinics, sometimes every single day. These protesters would engage in what they called 'kerbside counselling', except that it was nothing of the sort. It was abusive, shaming, an invasion of the privacy of a person seeking to use a lawful medical service. The reports of people having abuse screamed at them as they attended the clinics could not be ignored, nor could the people who said they were being filmed as they entered and exited the clinics, and who were worried that this material would be posted online.

The staff who worked at these health centres also endured this behaviour every day, and the security guards who were in attendance, as well as council by-law officers and police, were often called. The memory of Steve Rogers was no doubt at the forefront of many people's thoughts. Rogers was working as a security guard at an East Melbourne clinic that performed abortions in July 2001 when he was murdered by an anti-abortion activist, who intended to kill everyone who worked there and in other clinics as well. On reflection, I regret that it took so long for better protections to be put in place.

When the legal limitations of a reliance on council by-laws to try and deal with these pro-testers was highlighted, calls for new laws to establish safe-access zones got louder. Eventually, the *Public Health and Wellbeing Amendment (Safe Access Zones) Act 2015*, which took effect from May 2016, established a 150-metre zone around clinics and other health services in which activi-ties and communications about abortion designed to cause distress and anxiety were prohibited.

The introduction of the associated bill infuriated many. Those representing the churches claimed the bill would lead to the arrest of priests giving sermons in opposition to abortion. Those representing denominational organisations claimed they could not teach the biblical basis of their disapproval of abortion without the risk of being locked up. None of this was true, of course, and I did all I could to assure these organisations that their concerns were legally and practically misplaced; assertions concerning my own 'lost morality' that were put directly to me by opponents of the bill were not effective. And while a lot of what was said was really a proxy debate about abortion, and there were occasional frustrations, these discussions were, on the whole, respectfully had.

With some insignificant exceptions, the parliamentary debate on this issue was one of those experiences where people respectfully shared their passionate approval, opposition and dilemmas in coming to a view, and ultimately the bill was very widely supported. Given that the focus of the legislation was a lawful medical service, denying safe and dignified access to clinics would be unreasonable, many concluded. That left legitimate questions about practicalities, and exactly what was prohibited and what was lawful—all reasonable issues to raise. Many MPs actually shared personal stories or stories relayed from their constituents, which prompted the debate to transcend the binary template that characterises a lot of our performative parliamentary contributions. A colleague who had been an active participant in the movement to decriminalise abortion emphasised to me how different the tone and tenor of this debate had been in contrast to the 2008 debates. When I asked what had changed, what the difference was, my colleague observed that it was the power of personal stories—of parliamentarians genuinely reflecting on the very human impacts of the anti-abortion behaviours, putting themselves in the shoes of those who were having abuse hurled at them, and of those who walked into their workplace every day wondering if the person rushing at them had a gun.

The first person who was charged with breaching the safe-access zone laws, perhaps predictably, appealed, taking the legal challenge all the way to the High Court. The basis of the appeal was that the new laws were unconstitutional because they impermissibly burdened the implied freedom of political communication. The appeal was dismissed and the constitutional validity of the laws was upheld. The High Court found that the purpose of the laws was compelling and that any restriction of political communication in this case was valid.

These laws were a significant milestone for those who had endured battles outside women's health services for a long time. The staff at one these clinics invited a cross-party political group comprising those who had worked on these reforms to a Saturday night event to mark the occasion of the bill being passed. The following week, the parent of a child at my daughter's primary school told me my daughter had claimed in class that she had been to a 'cocktail party at an abortion clinic'. I had to confirm that this was true. 'Thought so,' the parent replied with a wry smile.

THE HUMANITY IN SHARING PAIN

Another example of a debate that demanded deep respect was when the Victorian Parliament considered the Voluntary Assisted Dying Bill in 2017. I am very proud of the fact that Victoria is the first state to have fully legalised assisted dying. The Northern Territory did pass and implement this momentous reform in the mid-1990s—assisted dying was legal there between 1996 and 1997—but the Commonwealth Government then overturned this law and removed the right of the Northern Territory to legislate. Two decades later, the Victorian Parliament passed the *Voluntary Assisted Dying Act 2017*. As other jurisdictions consider and legislate similar reforms, the nation will inevitably demand similar choices.

Much has been written and will continue to be written about this issue, including its medical and political history and the extraordinary advocacy of the proponents of voluntary assisted dying. Let me firmly place on the record my deep and admiring respect for all of those who carried the case for reform for so many long and lonely years. It was one of the great honours of my life to be part of the large and diverse team who helped make history in Victoria by delivering a compassionate and safe model that gives terminally ill people greater choice concerning how they die. I hope the momentum for this legal change that is gathering across the nation continues to find people of courage and tenacity to pursue it.

I want to emphasise the respect that fermented in the course of debating this issue, and to make the case that personal vulnerability in confronting something as universal as death helped those of us who were involved stay focused on our collective and individual humanity. This created a culture of respect for the feelings, wishes and rights of others. Again, there were exceptions to this when our passions got the better of us, myself included. Overwhelmingly, however, it was, in my experience, parliament at its finest.

Reforms to change the laws relating to end-of-life issues had never before made their way into both houses of parliament in Victoria. However, the members of a cross-party parliamentary committee immersed themselves in examining the then status quo of unregulated palliative sedation; terminally ill people taking their own lives in lonely, sometimes violent circumstances; the fact that not all end-of-life pain can be treated, and holding that up against international models that had been in operation for over thirty years without controversy. Around this time, the personal experiences of death of some members of parliament emboldened the sense that a respectful and considered process for instituting legalised assisted dying was possible. This changed everything, and the moment was seized.

A panel of medical, palliative, nursing and legal experts, led by the neurosurgeon and former Australian Medical Association president, Professor Brian Owler, worked tirelessly to take the recommendations of the parliamentary committee and flesh out and resolve the policy dilemmas. This intensive work led to even more intensive work by those charged with drafting the legislation before it was introduced into parliament—the legislation had to be crafted to support the right system, not the other way round. So the panel's task was to utilise their expertise to develop a model that would, in both clinical and ethical terms, work effectively and safely—the government had already agreed, for example, that any health professional who had a moral objection was not required to participate in supporting a terminally ill patient who was seeking assessment for an assisted death. In the end, it was clear that the panel experts did brilliant, quality work, based on being thought-ful, compassionate and persuasive. Being held in high regard professionally was a big help too—the panel members were respected and therefore their work was also respected. Expertise really does matter, particularly when it comes to reforms that are 'firsts'.

As the campaigns from opponents of the reform heated up, the fight over facts assumed great politi-cal importance. Doing justice to the consideration of a reform that is about life and death, that can invoke feelings of private pain, is quite a respon-sibility. The overwhelming majority of MPs took this responsibility incredibly seriously. Those who were pre-existing passionate supporters of end-of-life law reform wanted to understand why some of the eligibility criteria were very tight and the processes seemingly quite challenging for anyone trying to comply with them. Those who were vehemently opposed exercised their entitlement to critically examine the model. The parliamentarians who were unsure or open-minded, but who had their own questions, benefited from hours of briefings and bilateral conversations, talking through their concerns.

The public debate itself intensified in the lead-up to the parliamentary debate. Flyers appeared under windscreens in church car parks. Homilies opposing the reform were given by religious leaders and even some health professionals. In arguing for the reforms, many families, nurses, paramedics and doctors shared stories about the awful experiences of patients for whom they had cared. Email inboxes were bombarded, mainly by religious organisations. Go Gentle, a pro-reform organisation, was established by the well-known campaigner

Andrew Denton, lobbying and producing confronting material in its quest to win support for the bill. But the most powerful and impactful advocacy came from those who were terminally ill. Their testimony in community meetings, in the media, in one-on-one discussions with decision-makers, was simply too moving too ignore. Who the hell were we to deny them the possibility of managing their pain and their goodbyes when their lives were about to end?

The strain of being constantly lobbied began to show as some of my peers shut down, declining requests to meet with advocates and opponents. But many continued to cautiously reach out with practical, legal and ethical questions. Enabling the respected, experienced and thoughtful members of the expert panel to individually engage with these parliamentarians helped ensure we were then dealing with facts rather than just people's belief systems. Many, but not all, of those who sought private, quiet briefings, and the space to reflect on the different dimensions of the debate, voted for law reform. Those who did not vote in support of the bill held passionate and authentic objections. Of course, there were examples of standard political concerns, such as implied career consequences and incentives, and many Trojan Horse arguments. However, respect for expertise, for facts, for human experiences and reflection, enriched the debate. It helped us to make informed decisions and to seek to understand those who took an opposing view to our own, no matter how much we disagreed with it.

I met with many representatives of faith organisations who objected to the bill. Some of these meetings were more spirited than others—we all had a lot to lose. One faith leader asked to meet with me one-on-one, keen to have a broader conversation about the value of life, the state of global politics and poverty, how we both understood the concept of suffering. We knew we would not change each other's minds, but it was still a magnificent and, at least for me, therapeutic discussion. He left me with an album by the American cellist Yo-Yo Ma, asking me to listen to it and continue to reflect on what we had talked about.

I did. It helped me better understand the views of people I had disagreed with in that debate. I have the highest regard for the compassion and wisdom of this faith leader. And I still listen to the album he gave me, though via a streaming service now— even Yo-Yo had to move with the times.

When I was briefing and lobbying parliamentarians in support of the assisted dying reform, many generously shared deeply private memories with me. I learnt how indelible is the experience of watching a loved one die, how profoundly affected some people have remained even thirty or forty years later. As was reflected on in this debate many times, we are a death-denying society and most of us find talking about death and expressing grief awkward and uncomfortable.

Politicians are socialised to showcase a supposedly superior strength, an omnipotence against their opponents (internal and external). Showing vulnerability is associated with exposing a weakness, and in politics, all weaknesses are exploited. Despite all of the vulnerability literature, the TED Talks, the Brené Brown Instagram tiles, the modest improvements in the diversity of parliaments, it is still a risk-laden exercise for politicians to open right up and trust in an empathetic response from colleagues, constituencies and the media. But in the course of the parliamentary debates I have just described, people did reveal their greatest pain: the loss of people whom they had loved so deeply. They cried for their own loss, and they cried for the losses of others: for goodbyes never said, grandchildren never met, lives cut too short, adulthoods never reached. They expressed visceral pain, without embarrassment. They talked about the unspeakable guilt of being unable to legally respond to the begging wishes of a dying loved one, feeling they had deprived that person of a final sense of dignity.

In the midst of this bipartisan collegiality and respect, many parliamentarians expressed how torn they felt in determining a position. So many had submerged themselves in the debate and real-world experiences. Some argued their conscience would not allow them to support the bill. Some argued they were personally opposed to assisted dying but could not in good conscience deny that choice to others. Most argued that we had done the work required to develop a safe and secure model and that the status quo was unacceptable. Never before or since, in my experience, has a bill been so scrutinised, throughout the longest debate in the Victorian Parliament.

The bill was passed on 29 November 2017 and is now law in Victoria. The world has not fallen into an amoral abyss since then, as some predicted. Rather, parliamentarians, in revealing their pain and vulnerability, with no guarantee that this would not be exploited, had demonstrated many moments of beauty.

~

Assisted dying reforms have long been close to my heart and my home. Not long after I was born, my mum was diagnosed with multiple sclerosis, a terribly cruel disease to strike a 33-year-old woman with a tribe of kids and not a lot of money. My mum was a legend in how she got on with life, dealing with the limitations, the pain and the bloody unfairness of it all. Nevertheless, forty years of MS left her needing the highest level of care— she had become permanently bed-ridden, weighed about 34 kilos, had to put up with catheters and skin tears, was unable to digest food properly, and largely had all the joys of life taken away from her. Thank God for whiskey and horse racing, the welcome props in her week.

Us kids all grew up with the traditions and teachings of Irish Catholics—hence the whiskey. But there were some exceptions. My mother was definitely a progressive on things like contraception. 'Use birth control or you'll be poor like us,' she would counsel me after we had endured a sermon from the parish priest on the evils of birth control. And because she knew what the end of her life would be like with MS, she was an advocate for assisted dying reforms. There were many tortured moments when my mum urged that steps be taken to allow her to die. It was all just too much, and she had, all my life, indicated that this was what she would like to do. She followed the work of people like Dr Rodney Syme and other 'heroes' who argued for greater dignity in death. I, of course, did not want my mum to die—not then, not ever. But I knew that she knew her own mind, that she understood what was coming for her. She had endured over four decades of this bastard of a disease.

By this stage, it was impossible for her to end her life by herself. She couldn't even push tablets out of their plastic bubbles to stockpile them. She could only move with the help of a lifting machine, which always involved significant risks. She couldn't swallow all that much either. But the state of the law at the time meant that anyone who assisted her in dying would be committing a criminal offence— not really a great look if you are a lawyer or the minister for health (or a medical professional, as were some of my other family members). So there was a quiet, heartbreaking determination in my support to get this law changed. Each week, my mum would request updates and balefully shake her head as I talked about the next hurdle we faced. She agreed to have her story told to the media to showcase one of the very normal (and sweet) faces of those who needed us to get this done.

I like to think that when I introduced the Voluntary Assisted Dying Bill into the Victorian Parliament on 21 September 2017, there were many people clinking whiskey glasses in the heavens in celebration. If that happened, I know my mum was one of them. Sadly, she had not had the chance to experience the joy of making progress on this issue: she had died on 21 August, the day before her birthday. Four sad weeks after her death, my dad sat in the chamber to listen to my second reading speech, with some other lovely supporters patting him on the back. Literally carrying a mother lode of grief, we all just got on with it. There were many broken hearts amidst the advocates for reform— mine was just the most recently broken one. I kept the voice and encouragement of my mum with me at each tack and turn. With all of the afflictions of grief, and a little bit of what Joan Didion calls magical thinking, I just had to keep going, as success was in no way assured. There would be time for whiskey at the end.

It seems pretty obvious to say that standing in the shoes of other people helps us gain respect for their experiences. But so too can sharing from our own lives, asking for respect through the sheer expression of own vulnerability, taking the risk it may not be granted. That is what we can do to create a more humane body politic: keep displaying and requesting respect for all.

ACKNOWLEDGEMENTS

Louise Adler is a woman not to be messed with. Thank you, Louise, for eventually wearing me down to reflect on and commit to print my optimism about, and frustrations with, modern politics. Thank you to Paul Smitz for copyediting this book in a way that enabled it to make sense without eliminating my sass.

To Monash University, a place where I learnt to apply (some) academic rigour to my political passion, thank you for your support for, and investment in, the In the National Interest series. The world feels a little groundless sometimes, and ideas are not indulgences. Your commitment to this project in tough times is testament to your values.

My thanks and respect to my parliamentary colleagues, especially to Premier Andrews—I appreciate your leadership, trust and support, and it was a great honour to be part of your commitment to climbing the dangerous mountain of law reform that everyone said could not be scaled. To the public servants, the health and justice staff, who worked so tirelessly to improve services and achieve law reform, my deep thanks. My love and thanks to my team, especially my Chief of Staff, Chris McDermott. You could all have had an easier life. Thank you for choosing a challenging and interesting one instead.

Thank you to the advocates, the patients, the agents of change and justice, for the life lessons, the inspiration, and tenaciously arguing for a better, more decent, just and dignified life. Your support means the world. I hope the benefits outweigh the costs.

Big thanks to my extended family, but especially to my Bernie and my beautiful and smart daughters, Lily-Rose and Ginger. And to Mum and Dad, whose absence I feel every day. They started all the trouble by encouraging me to be educated, sceptical and kind, and to bring a good sense of humour everywhere you go in life.

NOTES

1   Claire Cain Miller, 'How to Be More Empathetic', *The New York Times*, n.d., https://www.nytimes.com/guides/year-of-living-better/how-to-be-more-empathetic (viewed March 2021).

2   'Collingwood President Eddie McGuire Says Release of Racism Report Is "a Historic and Proud Day" for Club', ABC News, 1 February 2021, https://www.abc.net.au/news/2021-02-01/eddie-mcguire-collingwood-report-racism-day-of-pride/13108980 (viewed March 2021).

3   Lorena Allam and Mike Hytner, 'Collingwood AFL Club's Culture of "Structural Racism" Condemned in Scathing Report', *The Guardian*, 1 February 2021, https://www.theguardian.com/sport/2021/feb/01/collingwood-afl-clubs-culture-of-structural-racism-condemned-in-scathing-report (viewed March 2021).

4   Ibid.

5   Michelle Grattan, 'Liberal MP Julia Banks to Quit at Election, Calling out Bullying', The Conversation, 27 November 2018, https://theconversation.com/liberal-mp-julia-banks-to-quit-at-election-calling-out-bullying-102340 (viewed March 2021).

6   Kathleen Calderwood, 'Brittany Higgins to Pursue
    Complaint of Rape in Parliament Office with Australian
    Federal Police', ABC News, 15 February 2021, https://
    www.abc.net.au/news/2021-02-15/brittany-higgins-
    parliament-house-rape-allegations/13157168 (viewed
    March 2021).

7   Royal Commission into Institutional Responses to
    Child Sexual Abuse, *Final Report*, 15 December 2017,
    https://www.childabuseroyalcommission.gov.au/
    final-report (viewed March 2021).

8   Royal Commission into Family Violence, *Report
    and Recommendations*, March 2016, http://rcfv.
    archive.royalcommission.vic.gov.au/MediaLibraries/
    RCFamilyViolence/Reports/RCFV_Full_Report_
    Interactive.pdf (viewed March 2021).

9   Cameron Wilson, 'Videos of People Refusing to Wear
    Masks Are Going Viral', ABC News, 28 July 2020,
    https://www.abc.net.au/news/science/2020-07-28/
    face-masks-bunnings-viral-video-covid19-
    coronavirus/12496434 (viewed March 2021).

10 SBS News, 'Julia Gillard's Misogyny Speech',
    October 2012, https://www.facebook.com/sbsnews/
    videos/264534671469298 (viewed March 2021).

11 Australian Associated Press, 'Victoria Bans Gay Con-
    version Practices after 12-hour Debate', 5 February
    2021, https://www.theguardian.com/australia-
    news/2021/feb/05/victoria-bans-gay-conversion-
    practices-after-12-hour-debate (viewed March 2021).

IN THE NATIONAL INTEREST

Other books on the issues that matter: